Kentucky Monthly

Coloring Book

Kentucky Monthly Coloring Book

Drawings
by Robert A. Powell

Digital Graphic Conversion
By Karen Sue Powell & Robert A. Powell

www.kyhawke.com

Published & Distributed by:

Vested Interest Publications

Frankfort, Kentucky 40601

ISBN 978-0-692-78810-3

Stephen M. Vest,
Editor and Publisher
Kentucky Monthly

Kentucky Monthly has always said they're about celebrating "the best Kentucky has to offer" and what better combination could we have than iconic images of our Commonwealth penned by noted Kentucky artist **Robert A. Powell.**

Coloring books are currently the rage and it's been our honor to work with Mr. Powell on putting together a collection that will excite Kentuckians from coast to coast. We have strived to include all parts of Kentucky, both east and west and north and south.

Based in Frankfort, Kentucky Monthly strives to unite Kentuckians wherever they may be and by highlighting the best our state has to offer, we create a sense of pride and community. We publish 10 issues per year, covering a wide variety of topics including travel, history, home, human interest, entertainment, outdoors, opinions, education, health, the arts, science and more.

Sincerely,
Stephen M. Vest, *Editor and Publisher*

Table of Contents

Kentucky Hawk 6

Ashland 9

Audubon Museum 11

Axe Lake Swamp 13

Belle of Louisville 15

Blackberry & Butterflies........ 17

Brown-Lanier House 19

Cannon at Cumberland Gap 21

Cardinal on Goldenrod......... 23

Chained Rock...................... 25

Coal Miner......................... 27

Columbus-Belmont.............. 29

Constitution Square 31

Corvette at Stone fence........ 33

Cumberland Falls................. 35

Duncan Tavern 37

Flat Lick Falls...................... 39

Floral Clock......................... 41

Fort Harrod........................ 43

Gazebo at Kingdom Come... 45

Gold Vault at Fort Knox........ 47

Gray Squirrel...................... 49

High Bridge........................ 51

Kentucky Capitol................. 53

Kentucky Derby................... 55

Kentucky Long Hunters........ 57

Kentucky Spotted Bass 59

Lake Cumberland................. 61

Lincoln Heritage House........ 63

Mainstrasse Clock Tower 65

McHargue's Mill................... 67

My Old Kentucky Home 69

Natural Bridge 71

Old Smokey 73

Perryville Battlefield 75

Springfield 77

Switzer Covered Bridge......... 79

Talbott Tavern 81

Thoroughbred Horses 83

Tulip Poplar........................ 85

UK Administration Building .. 87

Valley View Ferry................. 89

Weisenberger Mill 91

Whitehaven......................... 93

William Whitley House.......... 95

Wolf Pen Mill....................... 97

Subject Descriptions............ 99

ASHLAND

Home of Henry Clay ★ Lexington

AUDUBON MUSEUM

Henderson

AXE LAKE SWAMP

Barlow Bottoms ★ Ballard County

BELLE of LOUISVILLE
Riverfront ★ Louisville

BLACKBERRIES & VICEROY BUTTERFLIES

State butterfly ★ State fruit

BROWN-LANIER HOUSE

Mill Springs Battlefield ★ Monticello

CIVIL WAR CANNON
Cumberland Gap ★ Middlesboro

CARDINAL on GOLDENROD

State bird ★ State flower

CHAINED ROCK
Pine Mountain ★ Pineville

KENTUCKY COAL MINER

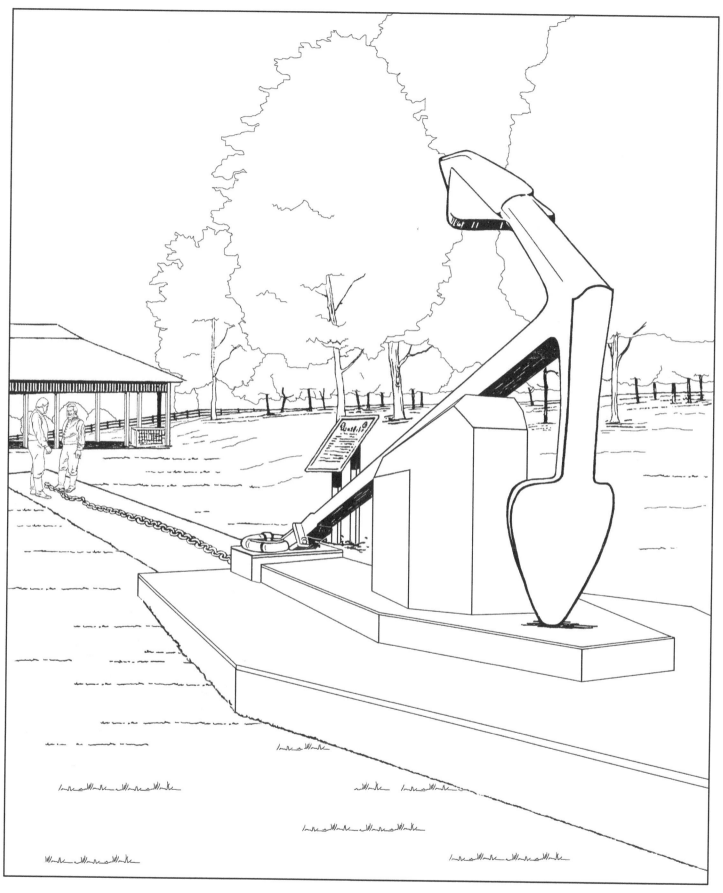

COLUMBUS-BELMONT

Civil War Park ★ Hickman County

CONSTITUTION SQUARE

Danville

CORVETTE

State sports car ★ Stone fences of the Bluegrass

CUMBERLAND FALLS
Corbin

DUNCAN TAVERN
Daughters of the American Revolution ★ Paris

FLAT LICK FALLS

Gray Hawk ★ Jackson County

FLORAL CLOCK
Frankfort

FORT HARROD

Harrodsburg

GAZEBO

Kingdom Come Park ★ Harlan County

GOLD VAULT
Fort Knox ★ Hardin County

GRAY SQUIRREL
State wild animal

HIGH BRIDGE
Over the Kentucky River ★ Jessamine-Mercer counties

KENTUCKY CAPITOL
Frankfort

KENTUCKY DERBY
Churchill Downs ★ Louisville

LONGHUNTERS
At Fort Boonesborough

SPOTTED BASS
State fish ★ Kentucky Spotted Bass

LAKE CUMBERLAND

Jamestown

LINCOLN HERITAGE

Freeman Lake ★ Elizabethtown

CLOCK TOWER
Mainstrasse Village ★ Covington

McHARGUE'S MILL

Levi Jackson ★ London

MY OLD KENTUCKY HOME

Federal Hill ★ Bardstown

NATURAL BRIDGE
Slade

OLD SMOKEY
Nicholasville

CIVIL WAR BATTLEFIELD

Perryville

SPRINGFIELD
Home of Zachary Taylor ★ Louisville

SWITZER COVERED BRIDGE

State covered bridge ★ Franklin County

TALBOTT TAVERN
Bardstown

THOROUGHBRED HORSES
State horse

TULIP POPLAR
State tree

MAIN BUILDING
University of Kentucky Administration Building ★ Lexington

VALLEY VIEW FERRY
Valley View on the Kentucky River

WEISENBERGER MILL

Midway

WHITEHAVEN
Paducah

WILLIAM WHITLEY HOUSE

Sportsman Hill ★ Lincoln County

WOLF PEN MILL

Jefferson County

Brief Subject Notes

Ashland is the magnificent home near Lexington built in 1805 by statesman Henry Clay. He was born April 12, 1777, in Virginia, came west as a young man, married Lucretia Hart and settled to make his mark in history. He and Lucretia lived at Ashland for many years, where they reared their 11 children. Clay was actively engaged in law and politics all his life, serving as a representative, U.S. Senator, Secretary of State and three times a candidate for President. He died in Washington June 29, 1852, and was returned for burial in the Lexington Cemetery with pomp and circumstance the nation had never seen. *Ashland* was named a national shrine on April 12, 1950, exactly 173 years after Henry Clay's birth.

John James Audubon State Park is a 692-acre wildlife sanctuary donated by the citizens of Henderson, in memory of the ornithologist and artist who roamed through the state from 1808 to 1826. He lived in Henderson for several years, gathering material for his monumental *Birds of America*. The park includes Audubon's his favorite haunts. In the "French Garden" is a small pavilion and two birdbaths, which are formed from old millstones found on the site of his "infernal mill." The French Norman architecture style was chosen because of his French ancestry, and it permits the round tower on the museum that contains holes for nesting birds.

Axe Lake Swamp State Nature Preserve was originally dedicated in 1991 as 146 acres of wetlands to protect the rare bald cypress swamp along the Mississippi River in far-western Kentucky. An additional 312 acres added in 2001, increased the size of the preserve to 458 acres. Acquired with assistance from *The Nature Conservancy* and *Kentucky Heritage Land Conservation Fund,* this unique preserve represents the first steps for the commission in assisting with the long-term protection of the entire 3,000-acre Axe Lake Swamp wetlands that supports rare plant and animal species, and large numbers of migratory waterfowl seasonally.

The Belle of Louisville was placed on the *National Register of Historic Places* in 1972 and designated a National Landmark in 1989. Owned and operated by the city of Louisville, she is moored at the downtown wharf next to the Riverfront Plaza. The Belle gained most of her popularity and fame in the annual riverboat race that began an unparalleled tradition in 1963

(against the Delta Queen) and quickly became a favorite part of the annual *Kentucky Derby Festival*. Originally named the *Idlewild*, she was built by *James Rees & Sons Company* in Pittsburgh, Pennsylvania in 1914. She came to Louisville in 1931 as an excursion boat but was sold and renamed *Avalon* in 1947. She operated along the Mississippi, Missouri, St. Croix, Illinois, Kanawha, Ohio and Cumberland Rivers. In 1962, Jefferson County Judge Marlow Cook bought her at auction and brought her back to Louisville where she was totally refurbished and then re-christened **Belle of Louisville**. She is docked on the Louisville waterfront and has become a great icon of Kentucky heritage.

Blackberry was named the official state fruit in 2004. They are delicious raw and are also used in desserts, jams, seedless jellies and wine. Blackberries are a widespread group of species of berry native throughout the Northern hemisphere, usually with numerous (and very sharp) short curved spines on the plant shoots.

The Viceroy Butterfly became the official state butterfly of Kentucky in 1990. Viceroy butterflies look like Monarchs; the coloring and pattern are nearly identical. However, a viceroy has a black line across the postmedian hindwing. Viceroys are smaller than the Monarchs, and their flight is faster and more erratic. Viceroys do not migrate. They winter as larvae, rolled up in a leaf of their host plant. In the spring, they need about 15 days to complete the life cycle and become a butterfly. The rate of viceroy development will depend on spring temperatures.

The Brown-Lanier House was the home of the miller operating the grist mill at *Mill Springs Park*. The house served as a home, headquarters, and hospital before and after the *Battle of Mill Springs*, the first Union victory of the Civil War. Three Generals occupied the house, General Felix K. Zollicoffer C.S.A., General Manson Malone U.S.A. and General George H. Thomas, U.S.A. The Monticello Woman's Club and other organizations reactivated the 1817s mill with aid from the Kentucky Department of Highways. The overshot waterwheel is the world's largest still in operation. Mill Springs Mill is on the *National Register of Battlefields* and is one of 25 included on a special Endangered Battlefield list.

Canon Protecting Cumberland Gap - The Cumberland Gap was a natural invasion route into the South for the Union. It provided access to vulnerable railroads and valuable minerals in Tennessee and Virginia. For the South, the Gap was a gateway for an invasion of Kentucky. The possession of Cumberland Gap changed hands four times during the Civil War. The Confederates first fortified the Gap in August 1861. Union forces, under General Morgan, took the Gap in June 1862. Then the Confederates, under General Stevenson, evacuated the Union troops from the Gap in September 1862 as they moved through the area and pushed on into the Bluegrass. The final exchange came when General Burnside accepted the surrender of Confederate General Frazer in September 1863.

The **Northern Cardinal** was named official state bird of Kentucky in 1926. It is one of America's favorite songbirds. Cardinals are distinctive in appearance; male cardinals are a brilliant scarlet red, females a buffy brown with reddish wings - both have a jet-black mask, pronounced crest, and heavy bill. The cardinal sings nearly year-round, and the male aggressively defends his 4-acre territory. Northern cardinals breed 2-3 times each season. The female builds the nest and tends the hatchlings for about 10 days while the male brings food. The male then takes care of this brood while the female moves on to a new nest to lay a second clutch of eggs. The cardinal is designated as the state bird for seven states: Illinois, Indiana, Kentucky, North Carolina, Ohio, Virginia, and West Virginia.

Goldenrod was designated official state flower of Kentucky in 1926.

Chained Rock was created in the early 1930s when Pat Caton and a few Kiwanians got the idea to chain the rock that appeared as if it might come crashing down on the city of Pineville. A giant 3,000-pound chain was donated for the project by a coal company in Virginia. The chain was transported by mule power to the top of Pine Mountain in sections. The mules gave out and were assisted by the Kiwanians, local Boy Scouts, and the CCC. Atop the mountain, the chain was welded together and connected. Fifty husky men used a set of triple block and tackle ropes and the spike team of mules to tighten the chain. The job was accomplished on June 24, 1933, and the news of chained rock appeared in more than 6,000 newspapers.

The **Kentucky Coal Miner** is the primary reason that America developed as a world leader in the 20th-Century. Coal Miners represent the heritage of Kentucky as significantly as the pioneer. The long difficult struggle of the coal miner definitely dominates the heritage of eastern Kentucky. Although coal mining was a labor intensive, dangerous way to make a living, during the Industrial Revolution, miners came from more than 38 different countries to build new lives. In 1929 Kentucky was the fourth largest bituminous coal-producing state in the country, and the greater part of this output came from southeastern Kentucky. The decade from 1920 to 1930 marked the rise of the Kentucky mines, and the union was finally able to organize Kentucky miners into the United Mine Workers of America, led by John L. Lewis.

Columbus-Belmont Battlefield State Park is located on the banks of the Mississippi River, at the old site of Columbus in Hickman County. Originally called the *Columbus-Belmont Battlefield Memorial Park*, it became a part of the Kentucky State Parks System in 1934. A military post was formed here in 1804. A settlement sprang up and a courthouse and jail were built here in 1823. During the *Civil War*, the *Union* plan for conquest of the South involved the mighty Mississippi. To prevent that strategy, Gen. Leonidas Polk, C.S.A., seized and heavily fortified the bluff above Columbus. A great chain more than a mile long was stretched across the river to prevent passage by Union gunboats. The giant chain was attached to a 6-ton anchor from a sea-going vessel on the Kentucky shore, and 140 guns were placed to sweep the river. The Missouri bank of the river at Belmont was also held by Confederates

Constitution Square Historic Site is a 3-acre park and open-air museum in Danville. From 1937 to 2012, it was a part of the Kentucky state park system. Danville was established as the seat of government for Kentucky County of Virginia. In 1780, the settlers began their campaign to become a separate state. Conventions were called on almost a year-to-year basis until a constitution was written, adopted and Kentucky was admitted to the Union as the 15th state on June 1, 1792. Constitution Square is a shrine to independence. It is located on the actual site where the first constitution was written, with 3 replicas (courthouse, church and jail) of buildings which stood on the town square. The first post office west of the Allegheny Mountains was established at Danville in 1798. The original old log structure was restored and moved to be part of the Constitution Square State Park.

Corvette was designated as the official state sports car for Kentucky in 2010. The National Corvette Museum is located at 350 Corvette Drive in Bowling Green. The Corvette is parked in front of the famous rock fences of the Bluegrass. The Chevrolet Corvette car has been produced through seven generations. The first model, a convertible, was introduced at the GM Motorama in 1953 as a concept show car. Myron Scott is credited for naming the car after the type of small, maneuverable warship which is called a corvette. The Corvette is manufactured in Kentucky and is listed as the official sports car of the Commonwealth of Kentucky.

Cumberland Falls is perhaps the most famous natural landmark in Kentucky. It is located on the *Cumberland River* in the rugged hills near Corbin, where the river cuts its way over a rocky course. The *Falls,* 68 feet high and 125 feet across, has an average flow of 3,600 cubic feet of water per second. Immediately behind the curtain of water is a recess in the rock wall that makes it possible to go almost across the river through an arch formed of rock on one side and flashing water on the other. The most unique and famous feature of *Cumberland Falls* is the magnificent double moonbow. In the full moon, a spectrum formed in the midst of the falls is more beautiful than a rainbow. It is the only one to be seen in the Western Hemisphere. The 900,000-acre *Daniel Boone National Forest* encircles *Cumberland Falls State Park.*

Duncan Tavern was in continuous operation for more than 150 years. Four years before Kentucky became a state, Major Joseph Duncan built this magnificent 20-room Georgian structure as a combination inn and tavern. His son, Joseph Duncan, the fifth Governor of Illinois (1834-38), was born in this house in 1794. In 1790, Jacob Spears erected one of the State's earliest distilleries near here, and the whiskey was called *Bourbon* for the county. The Limestone spring water contributed to the distinctive flavor of Kentucky Bourbon. A main stopping place on the Maysville-Lexington stagecoach line, historians attributed Duncan Tavern as having served the first drink of Bourbon commercially. Fully restored in the 1950s by the *Kentucky Society of the Daughters of the American Revolution*, Duncan Tavern today serves as its headquarters, and is maintained as a historic shrine.

Flat Lick Falls is located near Gray Hawk in Jackson County. It is one of those spectacular natural features that drew thousands of pioneers into this wilderness wonderland in the late 1700s and early 1800s. One fourth of Jackson County (56,000 acres), is within the Daniel Boone National Forest, making it representative of Eastern Kentucky's unique mountain topography. One of the most beautiful attractions in the state, Flat Lick Falls is situated in a setting that is more scenic than either Niagara Falls or Cumberland Falls. The cliffs throughout the area are more intriguing than Natural Bridge and the rock structure is more intricate than Mammoth Cave. In the summer of 2009 volunteers helped lay-out and clear the trails, and began developing the property for hiking, camping, and other passive recreation.

Kentucky's Floral Clock is unique in all the world. It sits prominently behind the State Capitol, on the west lawn of the Capitol Annex in Frankfort. The face of the clock is 34 feet across, the planter weighs 100 tons. The pedestal is faced with Kentucky fieldstone. It takes as many as 20,000 plants to fill the clock. The clock itself is an unusual timepiece. The hands actually rest for more than 22 hours of the day. They move once every sixty seconds. The works contain a control mechanism that makes corrections every hour and resets the clock in case of power failure. The decor of the  clock changes with each of the seasons. The **Floral Clock** was dedicated May 4, 1961, during the administration of Gov. Bert T. Combs.

Fort Harrod was the first permanent settlement in Kentucky. In 1773 Governor Dunmore of Virginia sent surveyors into the vast wilderness to survey public land to be used in paying off veterans of the French and Indian War. One of these surveying parties was led by Thomas Bullitt and James Harrod. Early in 1774 Harrod and 31 other men returned to the site he had surveyed, and on June 6, 1774, a settlement called Harrodstown was laid out. Indians began to attack, and by the end of 1774 the cabins at Harrodstown were deserted. In March 1775 Harrod and 30 men occupied the cabins while they built the Fort on higher ground for a defensive arsenal. Women and children began to arrive in September of 1775. *Old Fort Harrod State Park* was created in 1927 (originally known as *Pioneer Memorial State Park).*

The **Stone Gazebo** is one of the most popular features at the **Kingdom Come State Park** in Harlan County, near Cumberland. This remarkable circular stone landmark is situated at the entrance to the park and offers a spectacular view of Black Mountain and the town of Cumberland below. Black Mountain, with an elevation of 4,400 feet, is the highest point in Kentucky. Originally known as *Raven Rock Park*, the park was developed and renamed in 1961 to honor the inspiration of John Fox, who popularized the area in *The Little Shepherd of Kingdom Come.*  This story was the first American novel to sell more than a million copies. The park is located midway along the *Little Shepherd Trail*, which runs 38 miles along the crest of Pine Mountain (east of Harlan to south of Whitesburg).

Gold Vault at Fort Knox - The U. S. Treasury Department Gold Depository is more commonly referred to as the Gold Vault. It is located adjacent to the Fort Knox military reservation in Hardin County. Built in 1936 of granite, steel, and concrete, the two-story building measures 105 by 121 feet. Now under jurisdiction of the Director of the Mint, the building contains a two-level vault with a door that weighs more than twenty tons. The vault holds bars of almost pure gold. Each bar weighs about 27 1/2 pounds and measures 7 x 3 5/8 x 1 3/4 inches. Guarded 24 hours a day by a rotation shift of personnel selected from different government agencies, no visitors are allowed to enter. The first gold came to the Depository by railroad in January 1937, and the initial series of shipments was completed in June 1937.

Gray Squirrel was designated the official state wild animal of Kentucky in 1968. The gray squirrel is a native mammal of the rodent family that has been in North America for over 37 million years. The eastern gray squirrel is most frequently seen east of the Mississippi River. In autumn, the gray squirrel spends each day gathering nuts and seeds and hiding them so it will have enough food to last through the winter. The squirrel buries food in hundreds of different locations. The squirrel cleans each nut or seed before it is hidden and leaves a scent that the squirrel can find later in the winter, even under heavy snow. Squirrels are responsible for planting more trees than humans. **Tulip Poplar** was designated official state tree of Kentucky in 1994.

High Bridge was first planned as a suspension bridge by John Roebling, designer of the famous Brooklyn Bridge in New York City. Huge stone towers were built to hold cables in 1851, but work on the bridge was abandoned during the Civil War. Construction was resumed by the Cincinnati Southern Railway, and it opened in 1877. The bridge was dedicated in 1879 by President Rutherford B. Hayes. The 275/308-foot tall and 1,125-foot bridge crosses the deep gorge of the Kentucky River between Jessamine and Mercer counties. It is the first cantilever bridge built on the American continent and became an immediate tourist attraction as the highest railroad bridge in the world. In 1911 the bridge was rebuilt using the same foundations and without stopping rail service. In 1929 the large twin towers were torn down by Southern Railroad to permit double tracks.

Kentucky Capitol was dedicated June 1, 1910. Frankfort was the first permanent capital created west of the Alleghenies after Kentucky was admitted as the 15th State of the Union in 1792. It is the fourth permanent structure built to house the offices of state government. The first three Capitols were built on the site in the center of town where the *Old Statehouse* now stands. The first two structures were destroyed by fire. In 1905, the *General Assembly* selected a 34-acre site for a new capitol across the river from the old one, away from the crowded downtown area. The cornerstone was laid June 16, 1906, and the Capitol was completed in 1910 at a total cost (land, construction, and furnishings) of $1,820,000. It was built entirely by hand and it is still considered one of the biggest bargains in public buildings in America.

Kentucky Derby is run the first Saturday of May each year at Churchill Downs. The Derby has run every year since 1875 when the 180-acre racetrack was first opened by Colonel M.

Lewis Clark, who was inspired by the race tracks in England. With some friends, he formed the Kentucky Jockey Club and built the course. In 1875, ten thousand people watched as **Aristides** won the first Kentucky Derby. The Derby soon became America's supreme racing event and the first leg of the ultra-prestigious Triple Crown of racing. Some 200,000 spectators crowd into the park for the Derby each year and millions around the world view the activities on television. Since 1904 the Derby winner has been honored with a blanket of American Beauty roses. It was dubbed *Run for the Roses* in 1925 by Bill Corum, a New York sports writer.

A **Longhunter** was an 18th-century explorer and hunter who made expeditions into the wilderness for as much as six months at a time. Most long hunts started in Virginia in October and ended toward the end of March or early in April. These hunters gathered information in the 1760s and 1770s that was critical to the early settlement of Kentucky. Daniel Boone was one of the most famous long hunters on the American frontier. His vivid accounts of his hunting exploits helped draw settlers to Kentucky. The most famous are remembered because they named the natural features they discovered. Numerous entities in Kentucky also bear the names of long hunters, including Boone County and Boonesborough, for Daniel Boone, and Harrodsburg, named for James Harrod. Kenton County is named for Simon Kenton.

Kentucky Spotted Bass was designated as the official state fish of Kentucky in 1956. The spotted bass is also called spotty, or spots in various fishing communities. It is a species of freshwater fish of the sunfish family and is native to the Mississippi River basin and across the Gulf states, from Texas through Florida. It is often mistaken for the similar and more common largemouth bass. The most convenient way to distinguish between a largemouth bass and a spotted bass is by the size of the mouth. A spotted bass resembles a largemouth bass in coloration but will have a smaller mouth. The Kentucky Spotted Bass can reach an overall length of 25 inches, reaching weights of up to 11 pounds, and can reach an age of at least seven years. It is noted for the rows of dark spots below the lateral line, which give it its common name.

Lake Cumberland was created with the completion of Wolf Creek Dam in 1951. It is considered to be the number one houseboating destination in the United States. Lake Cumberland has proven to be a big boost to the area with more than 60 million dollars earned each year due to tourism. However, the economy of the region has also been affected indirectly with business and industry related, such as houseboat construction. The lake, which is 101 miles long and over one mile across at the widest point, has 1255 miles of shoreline. It is also famous for Striped Bass fishing. The Dam was constructed across the Cumberland River in Russell County just south of Jamestown. Started in 1941, the dam was not completed until 1951, primarily due to delays created by World War II. The purpose of the Dam itself is for flood control, hydroelectric power, recreation, and water quality.

Lincoln Heritage House stands in Freeman Lake Park in Elizabethtown as a tribute to the family of Abraham Lincoln. Built in 1789, it is known as the *Lincoln Heritage House*, and was once the home of Thomas Lincoln, a resident of Hardin County for more than ten years. He helped Samuel Haycraft build a millrace on Valley Creek. He married Nancy Hanks in 1806 and they lived in a log cabin built in Elizabethtown. Their daughter Sarah was born there in 1808. Soon after, they moved to the Sinking Spring Farm where Abraham was born in 1809. Thomas took his family to Indiana in 1816. Two years later his wife died, and he came back to Elizabethtown to marry Sarah Bush Johnston, who reared young Abraham. The house was restored by the Hardin County Historical Society and opened to the public in 1973.

Carroll Chimes Bell Tower in Mainstrasse Village in Covington is locally known as the Pied Piper Tower. The tower was completed in 1979 and named for then governor Julian Carroll. This 100-foot German Gothic clock tower is designed to look like a traditional glockenspiel with animated figures. On the hour, the bells chime and mechanical figures move onto a balcony to act out the story of the Pied Piper of Hamelin. In the 1970s, Mainstrasse was designated a National Register Historic District and local businessmen proposed building on the community's heritage to create a tourist attraction reminiscent of small villages in Germany. The clock tower with animated figures was completed at that time, adding to the Old World charm of the neighborhood.

McHargue's Mill is one of the few watermills remaining in Kentucky. There were thousands built in the early 1800s and continued until the wide scale use of electricity made them obsolete. The old mills were a vital part of the daily living for the early frontier settler, but they were very seasonal. There was too much water in the flood season and too little in dry spells. The grain farmers took to the mill was ground between a round, flint-like stone on top that turned and a stationary stone underneath. Water rushing over or under the wheel powered the gears which turned the great grinding stone. A bushel of corn could be ground in five to fifteen minutes. McHargue Mill was first built in 1812 at another location and was reconstructed here as part of the *Levi Jackson Wilderness Road State Park.*

"My Old Kentucky Home" was adopted as the official state song in 1928. **Federal Hill**, the manor house for the great plantation of John Rowan in Bardstown was the inspiration for the ballad by Stephen Foster and the nucleus for the state park. This splendid mansion was completed in 1818. Rowan's cousin, Stephen Foster, made this the immortal symbol for Kentucky when he wrote "My Old Kentucky Home" during a visit in 1852. The song quickly captured the hearts of the entire nation as exemplifying the traditional character of the South. It became Kentucky's state song in 1928, some 64 years after Foster died at the young age of 37. Rowan served as Secretary of State, member of the U. S. Congress, judge of the Court of Appeals and U. S. Senator. He died in 1843, nearly ten years before his home became an international landmark.

Natural Bridge has exhilarated Americans long before the pioneers first discovered this wilderness. The entire area is covered with artifacts from civilizations that precede the modern Indians. According to the calculations made by several geologists, this stunning formation actually took more than one million years to form an arch over 78 feet in length and 65 feet high. It includes more than fifteen million pounds of suspended rock. The stone in the center is over 20 feet wide, and it is actually flat enough to serve as a bridge. The area was developed by the Louisville & Nashville Railroad around the turn of the century as a terminus for weekend train excursions from the city. The entire area was turned over to the state by L & N about 1926 to be cultivated as one of the four original state parks. The park has 2,400 acres in the Daniel Boone National Forest.

Old Smokey is the largest operational steam locomotive in the state of Kentucky. Its maiden voyage on May 24, 2008, delivered more than 600 tons of sand from Louisville to Lexington. Since 1973 the *R. J. Corman Railroad Group, LLC* has been providing the highest quality service to the railroad industry. Headquartered in Nicholasville, they have divisions in 19 other states, employing over 800 people. Richard J. Corman, a native of Nicholasville, began railroad construction after high school, and in a little over 35 years, he turned a company with a single backhoe into one of the nation's leading railroad service providers. The engine was built in China in 1986. It weighs 140 tons and can produce 2,000 horsepower. It underwent repairs at Corman's Lexington yard before starting service in Kentucky.

Perryville Battlefield embraces 98 acres in which there is a museum, monuments to both Union and Confederates, Gen. Bragg's headquarters, two shrines, gift shop and picnic facilities. A re-enactment of the battle is staged here in October each year. The Battle of Perryville during the Civil War is considered one of the most significant military events in Kentucky history. It happened Oct. 8, 1862, and was purely an accident. Fought in complete desperation by both sides, it is accounted as one of the most bloody engagements of the entire war. There were 16,000 Confederates in action, 3,396 casualties (510 killed, 2,635 wounded, 251 MIA). Union forces numbered 61,000, but only 22,000 were sent into action. Their loss was 4,241 (845 killed, 2,851 wounded and 515 captured or missing). The Confederates slowly retreated out of Kentucky, but neither side claimed a victory.

Switzer Covered Bridge, the historic bridge over North Elkhorn Creek in Franklin County, was designated the official state covered bridge of Kentucky in 1998. The bridge is 60 feet long, and eleven feet wide; resting on sturdy stone supports. The side walls stop about two feet from the edge of the roof. The contractor was George Hockensmith. Built about 1855 and restored in 1906, then closed to traffic in 1954. The bridge was again restored in 1997 after a flood swept the bridge off its foundation. The Switzer covered bridge was listed on the *National Register of Historic Places* in 1974

Springfield was the home of Zachary Taylor for more than 20 years. It was also the scene of his marriage in 1810, and the birthplace for five of his six children. Zachary Taylor was only eight years old when his family moved from Virginia to a farm near Louisville in 1785. The family began their new life in Kentucky in a small log house, but within five years built this brick house. Upon his death at the White House in 1850, President Taylor's body was brought back to rest in the family burial ground at Springfield. This later served as the nucleus of the *Zachary Taylor National Cemetery.* The house is basically the same today as it was at the time of Zachary Taylor's residence. Zachary Taylor actually lived in Kentucky twice as long as Abraham Lincoln and four times as long as Jefferson Davis, both of whom are considered favorite sons. Zachary Taylor is the only former President buried in Kentucky.

Talbott Tavern is the oldest Western stagecoach stop in America. This old tavern & inn in Bardstown operated from 1779 continuously until it burned in 1998. Bardstown was considered a major crossroads for travelers of the American frontier; its guestbook includes notables such as Abraham Lincoln, George Rogers Clark, Andrew Jackson, Henry Clay, Zachary Taylor, Stephen Foster, John James Audubon, and most other statesman, soldier, or explorer who passed through the state. King Louis Philippe arrived here on October 17, 1797, with two brothers and several other members of his touring court. This was their headquarters while seeing the New World. One of the members of the entourage painted the famous murals in the Old Talbott Inn.

The Thoroughbred became the official state horse of Kentucky in 1996. Thoroughbred is a breed of horse celebrated for speed and endurance. Thoroughbreds are best known as racehorses but are also popular in other equestrian sports such as polo, hunting, and eventing. Off the track, thoroughbreds are also used in police work as well as equine-assisted therapy. All thoroughbreds trace their lineage to three stallions brought to Great Britain from the Middle East over three-hundred years ago. Known as the "Foundation Stallions" they are the *Byerly Turk,* the *Darley Arabian,* and the *Godolphin Arabian.* They were bred to native horses to produce a breed that could sustain speed over an extended distance. All American thoroughbred pedigrees are documented in the *American Stud Book*, first compiled by Colonel Sanders Bruce of Kentucky in 1873.

Main Building at the University of Kentucky was dedicated February 15, 1882. It is the only survivor of the four buildings which originally housed *State College*. It was designed using

brick and stone work at a total cost of $81,000. Previous funding attempts had failed, so the State College President James Patterson pledged his entire personal wealth "as collateral" to see the project completed. The original Main Building featured a 157-ft high cupola with a clock and the "captain's walk" from the building's completion to 1919, when the roof took on a "gabled appearance" that characterized the structure from 1920 until the fire in 2001. It originally housed the campus offices and several classrooms. It was renamed the Administration Building in 1948. While the building was being renovated in 2001, it was extensively damaged due to fire. The UK Board of Trustees immediately approved a plan to restore the structure and add a fourth story at a cost of $17,350,000. It reopened in 2004.

Valley View Ferry dates back to 1785 - seven years before statehood. The ferry was established on land acquired by John Craig in 1780 and named for its location in picturesque Valley View. The town, located on the Madison County side of the river, has only 200 residents, but in the early days was a thriving river community larger than Lexington. Even with the vast development of modern bridges and roadways, Valley View Ferry has continued to be an important link serving Jessamine, Madison and Fayette Counties. It is operated jointly by the governments of Fayette, Jessamine and Madison counties, and there is no charge to the passengers.

Weisenberger Mill is located on the *South Elkhorn Creek* along the Woodford-Scott County line. The creek has provided the water to power the mill's twin turbines since the early part of the 1800s. Six generations of the Weisenberger family have operated the mill at the present location since 1865. August Weisenberger emigrated from Baden, Germany in 1862. He purchased the existing mill in 1865. Philip, his son, was the second generation to take over operation of the mill. The mill was rebuilt in 1913 by Philip, using rock from the original mill. In the early years, the primary mill products were soft wheat flour and white cornmeal. Through the years, as the customers demanded more, the output changed to the meet all the baking needs.

Whitehaven is a majestic landmark cherished by the people of Paducah and surrounding areas. The original mansion was a two-story brick structure, built in the 1860s by Edward Anderson. Edward Atkins bought it in 1903 and had noted Paducah architect A. L. Lassiter transform the Victorian farmhouse into a Classical Revival mansion. He added the Corinthian-columned front portico and named the house *Whitehaven*. In 1908, Paducah mayor James Smith bought and renamed his home *"Bide-A-Wee"*. Smith family members lived here until 1968. The restored 1860s Southern mansion features period furnishings and memorabilia of Paducah native Alben Barkley, who served as Vice-president under Harry Truman. It opened in 1983, as *Whitehaven Welcome Center* along I-24; the only historic house serving as an interstate welcome center.

William Whitley House is the oldest brick house in Kentucky. It was built in the 1780s by Col. William Whitley, who came to Kentucky from the more civilized part of Virginia in 1775. Often used as a haven of safety from roving Indians, they dubbed their fine residence "Guardian of the Wilderness Road." Over the front door, the letters WW for William Whitley are visible in brick of a lighter color. EW for his wife Esther Whitley is over the back door. The house passed out of the Whitley family after Colonel Whitley was killed at the *Battle of the Thames* in 1813. Both *Whitley County*, and the county seat of *Williamsburg* are named in his honor. Situated just southeast of Stanford, the *William Whitley House* is now a State Shrine.

Wolf Pen Mill is located in Jefferson County, some 11 miles from Louisville, near the Oldham County line. Although it was built in the mid-1830s, this old three-story stone building still rests on a brick-and-stone foundation with solid walls two feet thick, that were laid without mortar. The original roof was covered with long, hand split, white oak shingles, and the gable ends were weather-boarded. The old water-powered mill, with its 26-foot wooden wheel, is situated on Wolf Pen Branch and is fed by a millrace which goes around the back of the mill to the stream. Grinding was done on two sets of French buhrs, with one set of millstones that measured 4 1/2 feet in diameter.